AF228542

Oregon

BY DORIS EDWARDS

CONTENT CONSULTANT
David Peterson del Mar, PhD
Professor of History
Portland State University

Core Library

An Imprint of Abdo Publishing
abdobooks.com

abdobooks.com

Published by Abdo Publishing, a division of ABDO, PO Box 398166, Minneapolis, Minnesota 55439. Copyright © 2023 by Abdo Consulting Group, Inc. International copyrights reserved in all countries. No part of this book may be reproduced in any form without written permission from the publisher. Core Library™ is a trademark and logo of Abdo Publishing.

Printed in the United States of America, North Mankato, Minnesota.
052022
092022

Cover Photo: Shutterstock Images
Interior Photos: Kris Wiktor/Shutterstock Images, 4–5; Red Line Editorial, 7 (Oregon), 7 (USA); Emily Marie Wilson/Shutterstock Images, 10–11, 43; Christopher Chapman/Alamy, 14; Shutterstock Images, 17 (flag), 17 (flower), 39; Christian Musat/Shutterstock Images, 17 (beaver); Hugh K. Telleria/Shutterstock Images, 17 (tree); David Spates/Shutterstock Images, 17 (bird); iStockphoto, 19; Marisa Estivill/Shutterstock Images, 20–21, 45; Sara Winter/Shutterstock Images, 22; Tom Reichner/Shutterstock Images, 25; Robert Crum/Shutterstock Images, 28–29; Tada Images/Shutterstock Images, 32; Josemaria Toscano/Shutterstock Images, 34–35; Rick Bowmer/AP Images, 40

Editor: Marie Pearson
Series Designer: Joshua Olson

Library of Congress Control Number: 2021951575

Publisher's Cataloging-in-Publication Data

Names: Edwards, Doris, author.
Title: Oregon / by Doris Edwards
Description: Minneapolis, Minnesota : Abdo Publishing, 2023 | Series: Core library of US states | Includes online resources and index.
Identifiers: ISBN 9781532197789 (lib. bdg.) | ISBN 9781098270544 (ebook)
Subjects: LCSH: U.S. states--Juvenile literature. | Western States (U.S.)--Juvenile literature. | Oregon--History--Juvenile literature. | Physical geography--United States--Juvenile literature.
Classification: DDC 979.5--dc23

Population demographics broken down by race and ethnicity come from the 2019 census estimate. Population totals come from the 2020 census.

CONTENTS

THE BEAVER STATE

Hikers walk uphill through a meadow. The meadow gives way to a rocky rim. Below them Crater Lake's blue waters reflect the cliffs that surround it. A jagged, rocky island rises from the water. The island is called Phantom Ship. It is long and narrow like a ship. Across the lake a boat takes visitors to Wizard Island, the largest island in Crater Lake. Crater Lake is one of Oregon's natural wonders. It is surrounded by cliffs that stretch 2,000 feet (610 m) into the sky.

Crater Lake offers spectacular views.

At 1,943 feet (592 m) deep, it is the deepest lake in the United States and one of the deepest on Earth.

WILLIAM GLADSTONE STEEL

In the 1880s William Gladstone Steel was working at a post office in Portland. He decided to visit Crater Lake. He wrote about the lake in 1886, "An overmastering conviction came to me that this wonderful spot must be saved, wild and beautiful, just as it was, for all future generations, and that it was up to me to do something." Gladstone worked for years to make sure the government would protect the land. On May 22, 1902, President Theodore Roosevelt signed a bill into law. Crater Lake officially became a national park.

ABOUT OREGON

Oregon is part of the Pacific Northwest. This region has mountains, forests, and Pacific Ocean coastline. Oregon is just south of Washington State. The Columbia River makes up much of Oregon's border with Washington. To the west, the Pacific Ocean meets beaches and towering cliffs. Idaho forms the eastern border. California and

MAP OF
OREGON

Take a look at this map. How does it help you understand Chapter One's discussion about Oregon?

Nevada border Oregon to the south.

Oregon is known as the Beaver State. It got its nickname from the river mammal. In the 1800s fur hats were fashionable. French and British traders worked with American Indian people to trap beavers living in Oregon's rivers. European settlers ate beaver meat. They used beaver fur to make hats.

In Oregon, a big city and the quiet wilderness are equally fascinating. Large urban areas such as Portland,

Salem, and Eugene are in the west. Smaller cities and towns, including Medford and Bend, are scattered throughout the state. Several mountain ranges crisscross Oregon and often extend into neighboring states.

To the east, farms and ranches dot the state. In many parts of Oregon, tall mountains give way to high deserts. Hells Canyon is in eastern Oregon. It is the deepest canyon in the United States. Throughout Oregon, there are protected forests, rivers, and lakes. Its natural beauty brings many visitors each year.

EXPLORE ONLINE

Chapter One discusses Crater Lake. The website below goes into more depth on this topic. Does the website answer any questions you had about this natural wonder?

12 FACTS ABOUT CRATER LAKE

abdocorelibrary.com/oregon

HISTORY OF OREGON

eople lived in Oregon long before Europeans arrived. They began living in the region at least 12,000 years ago. Modern American Indian nations descended from these people. These nations traded with one another.

Coos, Lower Umpqua, and Siuslaw peoples lived in what is now southwest Oregon. Their territories extended from the ocean to the Coastal Range. These people fished, hunted, and gathered plants. They lived in sturdy houses made of cedarwood.

Clatsop, Chinook, Umatilla, and many other peoples lived along the Columbia River in northern Oregon. Common foods included salmon, elk, and berries. These people used canoes to travel on the water. They made different canoes for the river and the ocean.

The Siletz people have roots along the

central and northern Oregon coast. They lived in long houses made of cedarwood or pine boards. Some were more than 100 feet (30 m) long. Several families lived in a single house. The houses had fireplaces for cooking food.

EUROPEANS

European explorers may have first arrived in the mid-1500s. Historians think British sailors came in 1579. These sailors visited only the coast. They did not explore inland. The sailors traded with coastal American Indian people.

In the late 1700s, British traders came to the Pacific Coast. They were looking for fur. The fur trade was booming across the continent. Trappers worked with American Indians on the coast and inland. They hunted otters and beavers. People valued these animals' pelts. Companies used the pelts to make hats.

AMERICAN EXPLORERS AND SETTLERS

Some of the first American explorers were William Clark and Meriwether Lewis. In 1803 the US government bought a large area of land west of the Mississippi River. President Thomas Jefferson asked Lewis and Clark to explore the region and beyond. The group traveled along the Columbia River in 1805. Along the way, the group received help from several American Indian nations, including the Clatsop.

A growing number of white American settlers began arriving in the 1830s. Many were religious missionaries. Others wanted access to the fertile land in the west. At this time, the British and Americans both claimed Oregon. From the 1840s to the 1860s, hundreds of thousands of American families traveled to the area from the east. Most journeyed along the Oregon Trail. The route stretched 2,000 miles (3,200 km) from the Missouri River to the Oregon coast. The trip was difficult. Many people died.

By the mid-1840s, the fur trade had declined. As a result, the British no longer had interest in the region. They struck a land deal with the United States in 1846. The treaty gave the United States the Oregon Territory. This territory included present-day Oregon, Washington, Idaho, and parts of Montana and Wyoming.

In the late 1840s and into the 1860s, more white settlers came to explore the territory. Some were on their way to find gold in California. They forced

American Indians out of their lands. As a result, many American Indian nations signed treaties with the US government. These agreements created reservations for American Indians. Often these reservations were much smaller than their original lands.

STATEHOOD

On February 14, 1859, Oregon became the thirty-third state. It was carved from the Oregon territory. Gold was discovered earlier in this decade. It brought many people to the state, including people from China. More Chinese people came in the 1870s. They helped build a railroad. By 1890 Oregon had the second-largest Chinese population in the nation. Oregon was also the only state with exclusion laws that banned people of certain races from legally living, working, or owning property in the state. This practice dated to before statehood. Some laws prohibited Black people from entering Oregon. All of the exclusion laws were repealed in 1926. But to this day, Portland is one of the whitest major US cities.

OREGON
QUICK FACTS

Examine these facts and symbols of Oregon. How do you think each represents the state?

State flag (front)

Abbreviation: OR
Nickname: The Beaver State
Motto: She flies with her own wings
Date of statehood: February 14, 1859
Capital: Salem
Population: 4,237,256
Area: 98,379 square miles (254,800 sq km)

STATE SYMBOLS

State animal
Beaver

State flower
Oregon grape

State bird
Western meadowlark

State tree
Douglas fir

Today tribal nations on reservation lands receive money from the federal government as part of the treaty agreements. But in the 1950s, the government stopped funding for 109 American Indian tribes across the United States. Sixty-two were in Oregon. Some of these tribes worked to restore recognition. In the 1970s and 1980s, six tribes in Oregon were able to become recognized again.

STATE GOVERNMENT

Oregon's state government has three branches. The legislative branch has two groups of elected officials. Senators and representatives work

to create, change, and vote on new bills. Bills may become laws.

The executive branch includes the governor. The governor has the power to sign bills into law. The judicial branch includes Oregon's courts. The Oregon Supreme Court is the highest court. Courts interpret and apply laws in court cases. Oregon also has nine recognized tribes. These tribes have separate governments.

GEOGRAPHY AND CLIMATE

Oregon has several geographic regions. Each of these regions has unique landforms. These landforms affect climate. Plants and animals have adapted to live in these areas.

The Coast Range runs north to south along the Pacific Ocean. It is a chain of mountains. There are tall cliffs in the Coast Range. This area is filled with trees. Its location near the ocean means it has mild weather. Ocean water

Oregon has many scenic mountain and coastal views.

A dry lakebed in Alvord Desert is covered in cracked soil.

helps keep temperatures steady. This area gets a lot of rain throughout the year.

South of the Coast Range is the Klamath Mountains. This part of the state is covered with steep forests, gentle foothills, and flat valleys. Many rivers run through the area, including the Umpqua and Rogue Rivers. Because of the region's varied geography, the weather can range from rainy along the Pacific Ocean to dry in the valleys and freezing in the mountains.

The Willamette Valley is a narrow strip of land to the east of the Coast Range. It runs along the Willamette River, which flows north into the Columbia River. Here, the soil is rich. The climate is mild and great for growing crops.

Oregon's most famous mountains may be the Cascade Range. They are located east of the Willamette Valley and run north to south. This rugged, often snowy landscape is where many of the United States' highest peaks are found. Mount Hood is Oregon's highest point. It stretches 11,240 feet (3,426 m) into the sky.

The central and eastern areas usually have less rain and snow. The bordering Cascade mountains block moist ocean air from reaching inland. Summers are hotter and winters are colder than on the coast. In the southeast the Steens and Hart Mountains rise into the sky. Nearby basins and landforms include the Alvord Desert and Lake Albert. The area is known for its dry climate and high temperatures in the summer.

PLANTS AND ANIMALS

Many plants and animals live in Oregon's habitats. Oregon's most common tree is the Douglas fir. It is also the state tree. Native trees of eastern Oregon include the ponderosa pine, grand fir, and western juniper. Aspen trees on Steens Mountain turn shades of yellow and orange in the fall.

More than 400 species of birds live all over the state, including turkeys, vultures, and ospreys. Eastern Oregon is home to more than 15 million acres (6 million ha) of sage grouse habitat.

The greater sage grouse lives in the high desert of southeastern Oregon. The western meadowlark is known for its wonderful song. In 1927 it was chosen as the state bird by Oregon's schoolchildren.

GREEN STURGEON

The green sturgeon lives in and around oceans. It spends part of its life in salt water and part in fresh water. Sturgeons do not have scales like most fish. Instead, they have bony plates. Predators cannot bite through the plates. Sturgeons can grow up to 7 feet (2.1 m) long and weigh 350 pounds (160 kg)! These fish are big, but they are not aggressive. They eat small animals from the ocean floor, such as shrimp.

In the mountains, cougars, black bears, and various types of deer are common. Elk live throughout the state but are most often found in the Blue and Wallowa mountain ranges and the Coast Range.

Oregon's waters are also important habitats. Sea lions live in the ocean. They eat fish and shellfish. Rivers hold otters and salmon. The Chinook salmon is the largest of the Pacific salmon. Spotted frogs, Pacific giant salamanders, and coastal tailed frogs are just some of the state's amphibians.

STRAIGHT TO THE
SOURCE

The western meadowlark became Oregon's state bird in 1927. But in 2017 there was a failed move to change that. The western meadowlark is also the state bird for five other states. Many people thought the osprey should be Oregon's state bird instead. State Senator Elizabeth Steiner Hayward said:

The osprey is like Oregon. We are fierce. We are independent. We are [found all] across our state. You can find an osprey nesting along any body of water in this entire state whether it's urban or rural.

You can see osprey. They're big. They're obvious. They have a unique flight [pattern]. They're fascinating to watch, and they can engage people in a way that a small bird—that's tough to see— cannot engage people.

Source: Diane Dietz. "Oregon Senate Chooses the Osprey Over the Western Meadowlark as State Bird." *Statesman Journal*, 7 Apr. 2017, statesmanjournal.com. Accessed 16 June 2021.

WHAT'S THE BIG IDEA?

Read the above quote carefully. What is the main point Steiner Hayward is trying to make? What evidence does she use to support that point?

RESOURCES AND ECONOMY

Oregon's economy has changed over time. Originally the state depended on farming, fishing, and timber. From the mid-1800s to the mid-1900s, farmers in the western part of the state grew flax for making linen and hemp for paper. They planted orchards full of plums, walnuts, filberts, and other fruits and nuts. In the Columbia Plateau, wheat fields thrived. Ranchers raised cattle for meat.

Oregon has orchards for many kinds of foods, including apples.

PERSPECTIVES

WOMEN IN FISHING

In 1866 the first salmon cannery on the Columbia River opened. Many local men worked there. Robert Hume, one of the cannery's founders, wrote: "As we were located three miles [4.8 km] from the nearest neighbors, it was months before we got sight of any womankind, except my mother." At the time, most canneries in Oregon employed Japanese and Chinese men. Then in the late 1800s and early 1900s, that practice changed. White men and women were hired. Most of the men did the fishing. Both men and women did the canning and labeling. Women were paid less. In 1910 they made $1.50 per ten-hour day. Men made $2.50 for the same job.

During this time, the construction of railroads brought people to all parts of the state. They worked in the mining and timber industries. Logging increased as rail lines made the export of wood easier. By 1938 Oregon was the nation's top producer of wood. Oregon continues to produce more wood for building than any other state. Salmon fishing and canning were important industries in Oregon too.

BIG INDUSTRY

Most big cities in
Oregon are on the
western side of the
state. These cities
are home to many
types of industries.
In the late 1900s,
technology became
more important.
Companies attracted
thousands of people
to cities. For example,
technology companies
such as Intel opened
offices in the Portland
area in the 1970s
and 1980s. Over the
next 30 years, the number of people working in
these companies multiplied. The area became known

THE MIGHTY FISH LADDER

Located on the Columbia
River about 30 minutes from
Portland, the Bonneville Dam
is one of the world's largest
hydroelectric systems. It
produces 5 billion kilowatts
of electricity each year. This
provides power for 80 percent
of the Pacific Northwest. But
several species of salmon
need to swim back upstream
each year in order to lay
eggs. Engineers designed
fish ladders so they could get
past the dam. The fish ladders
help Chinook, sockeye,
coho, and steelhead salmon
swim upstream. Hundreds of
thousands of fish can pass
through in a single day during
August through November.

as the Silicon Forest. Silicon is a material used to make electronics.

Sports clothing and shoe companies also came to Oregon. Nike has its world headquarters there. Portland is home to Adidas's North American headquarters. Countries around the world buy goods from Oregon.

Oregon also has a massive tourism industry. People come from all over the world to visit its bustling cities and jaw-dropping scenery. In 2018 more than 29 million people visited the state. One of Oregon's biggest draws is the Willamette Valley. It is home to two-thirds of Oregon's grape vineyards.

CHANGING ENVIRONMENT

In the beginning of 2019, Oregon had a lot of job growth. Many people arrived in urban areas for work opportunities. This caused cities to grow.

Growing cities demand a lot of energy. Oregon is working to use its renewable resources to provide electricity. Electricity created by water, sun, and wind does not harm the environment as much as other methods of producing energy. Oregon has many large rivers. As a result, the state gets the majority of its electricity from hydropower.

FURTHER EVIDENCE

Chapter Four discusses how Oregon generates electricity from its rivers. Identify one of the author's main points. What evidence does the author provide to support this point? The article and video at the website below also discuss the topic. Find a quote on this website that supports the author's main point. Does it offer a new piece of evidence?

HYDROPOWER IN THE NORTHWEST

abdocorelibrary.com/oregon

PEOPLE AND PLACES

Oregon has a mix of cities and farms. These areas meet up with beautiful parks and wilderness areas. Though Salem is the state's capital, Portland is Oregon's largest city. The city and the surrounding communities make up approximately 60 percent of Oregon's population. However, rural areas take up the most land. Many of the rural communities are in eastern Oregon.

Mount Hood overlooks Portland.

BUILDING A BETTER PORTLAND

Bill Naito was born in Portland in 1925. He was Japanese American and faced anti-Asian racism growing up. After serving in the army in World War II (1939–1945), he returned to the city. He worked with his father and brother. They fixed up more than 20 historical buildings. In 1975 they turned an old warehouse into Portland's first downtown shopping mall. That same year, he and his family opened the first of many Made in Oregon stores. These stores sell a variety of products made in the state.

More than 4.2 million people live in Oregon. About 75.1 percent of Oregonians are white people who are not Hispanic or Latino, 13.4 percent are Hispanic or Latino, 4.9 percent are Asian, and 2.2 percent are Black. American Indian and Alaska Native people are 1.8 percent of the population.

Famous Oregonians include writer Beverly Cleary and actress Katee Sackhoff. Ashton Eaton is also from Oregon. He won gold medals for the decathlon in the 2012 and 2016

Olympics. Celebrated chef James Beard was from Oregon too. Born in Portland, he started his own cooking school. The James Beard Foundation Awards are given yearly to the best chefs in the United States.

NATURAL WONDERS

People do not need to leave the city to see nature. Forest Park is in Portland. It is one of the largest urban parks in the United States. It has gardens and 80 miles (130 km) of hiking trails. It is an important natural retreat for people who cannot drive out of the city.

Outside of the cities, the Eagle Cap Wilderness in the Wallowa Mountains has miles of hiking trails. On Oregon's northern coast, people can watch gray whales migrate from late February to May and from mid-December to mid-January. Winter sports including skiing and snowboarding are popular on the Cascades' snowy slopes.

A MOVE WORTH MAKING

In 1995 Anthony Heald was a successful actor on Broadway in New York City and was also a film actor. He was nominated twice for a Tony Award, including one for his lead role in *Love! Valour! Compassion!* But instead of continuing his career, he decided to leave New York. He moved to Ashland, Oregon. Since then he has performed in the Shakespeare Festival for many years. He said of how quiet audiences were during performances, "I've never performed for audiences that are at the level that they are in the three theaters in Ashland," Heald said. "There's a respect for the art."

ARTS AND SPORTS

For people looking for an art scene, Oregon has plenty to offer. One of the state's popular traditions is the Oregon Shakespeare Festival. Located in Ashland, the festival attracts more than 400,000 people from all over the world every year. People visit the city of Joseph from across the state to attend the Wallowa Valley Festival of Arts every September.

Sports are also popular. Oregon is

Oregon's mountains are popular places for snowboarding and other winter activities.

home to three major professional sports teams. From the 1970s to the 1990s, the Portland Trail Blazers were one of the most successful teams in the National

Basketball Association. The Portland Thorns FC are part of the National Women's Soccer League (NWSL). They won the 2013 and 2017 NWSL championships. The men's soccer team, the Portland Timbers, joined Major League Soccer (MLS) in 2011. They won the MLS Cup in 2015. Portland is still called Soccer City USA by many sports fans.

From its rugged landscapes to its bustling cities, Oregon is one of the most thrilling US states to visit. With its rich history and variety of things to do and learn, there's always something new to explore.

STRAIGHT TO THE
SOURCE

The Oregonian, the state's biggest newspaper, published a list of the top 50 natural wonders to visit in Oregon. The top spot went to the Wallowa Mountains. Reporter Jamie Hale wrote:

> *Isolated in the far northeastern corner of the state, the Wallowa Mountains are a place of incomparable beauty. The range is often called the "Swiss Alps of Oregon," but that comparison downplays the more unique features of the Wallowas: the marble-capped mountains, roaring turquoise rivers, towering waterfalls, alpine lakes and dense forests. Wallowa Lake at the base of the mountains is a gorgeous sight in and of itself, while the tramway that leads to the top of Mount Howard is a great manmade feature. There's nothing in Oregon quite like the Wallowas, a comprehensive display of pure natural awe.*

> Source: Jamie Hale. "Oregon's 50 Most Beautiful Places."
> *The Oregonian*, 29 Aug. 2019, oregonlive.com.
> Accessed 21 June 2021.

BACK IT UP

The author of this passage is using evidence to support a point. Write a paragraph describing the point the author is making. Then write down two or three pieces of evidence the author uses to make the point.

IMPORTANT DATES

12,000 years ago
People begin living in what is now Oregon at this time, if not earlier.

Mid-1500s CE
Europeans visit the coast of Oregon.

1800s
European trappers trade with American Indian people along the coast.

1805
Meriwether Lewis and William Clark lead an expedition that explores present-day Oregon.

1846
Oregon becomes a US territory.

1859
Oregon becomes the thirty-third state on February 14.

1926

Courts repeal the Oregon laws that prevent Black people from living in the state.

1950s

Sixty-two tribes in Oregon lose federal recognition.

2018

More than 29 million people visit Oregon.

STOP AND THINK

Tell the Tale

Chapter One describes visiting Crater Lake. Imagine you are exploring this lake. What do you see? What activities are there for you to do? Describe the experience in 200 words.

Dig Deeper

After reading this book, what questions do you still have about Oregon's history? With an adult's help, find a few reliable sources that can help you answer your questions. Write a paragraph about what you learned.

Take a Stand

This book describes big cities and small towns in Oregon. Think about these urban and rural areas in your state. How are they different from each other? Would you prefer to live in one over the other? Why?

Why Do I Care?

Maybe you aren't interested in learning about different work industries. But that doesn't mean you can't think about how the products affect your life. Think about the items that Oregon produces. How would your life be different without these products?

GLOSSARY

adapt
to change over time to develop a feature or skill that helps an animal or plant survive

civil rights
rights that people have for personal freedom

export
to ship and sell products to another region or country

habitat
the place where a plant or an animal lives

hydropower
electricity that is created by moving water

pelt
an animal's skin and fur

prohibit
to not allow or to ban something

repeal
to cancel or reverse

rural
having to do with the countryside

treaty
an official agreement between governments

urban
relating to a city environment

ONLINE RESOURCES

To learn more about Oregon, visit our free resource websites below.

Visit **abdocorelibrary.com** or scan this QR code for free Common Core resources for teachers and students, including vetted activities, multimedia, and booklinks, for deeper subject comprehension.

Visit **abdobooklinks.com** or scan this QR code for free additional online weblinks for further learning. These links are routinely monitored and updated to provide the most current information available.

LEARN MORE

Moussavi, Sam. *Portland Timbers*. Abdo, 2022.

O'Brien, Cynthia. *Encyclopedia of American Indian History and Culture.* National Geographic, 2019.

INDEX

About the Author

Doris Edwards lives in Portland, Oregon. She has written many books for young readers. When she isn't writing, you can find her gardening or baking tasty cookies for her grandkids.